Albion's glory: a pindarique ode
on the royal train that attended
the happy coronation of Her most
sacred Majesty Queen Ann. Written
by the authors of Britannia's loss.

Gale ECCO Print Editions

Relive history with *Eighteenth Century Collections Online*, now available in print for the independent historian and collector. This series includes the most significant English-language and foreign-language works printed in Great Britain during the eighteenth century, and is organized in seven different subject areas including literature and language; medicine, science, and technology; and religion and philosophy. The collection also includes thousands of important works from the Americas.

The eighteenth century has been called "The Age of Enlightenment." It was a period of rapid advance in print culture and publishing, in world exploration, and in the rapid growth of science and technology – all of which had a profound impact on the political and cultural landscape. At the end of the century the American Revolution, French Revolution and Industrial Revolution, perhaps three of the most significant events in modern history, set in motion developments that eventually dominated world political, economic, and social life.

In a groundbreaking effort, Gale initiated a revolution of its own: digitization of epic proportions to preserve these invaluable works in the largest online archive of its kind. Contributions from major world libraries constitute over 175,000 original printed works. Scanned images of the actual pages, rather than transcriptions, recreate the works *as they first appeared.*

Now for the first time, these high-quality digital scans of original works are available via print-on-demand, making them readily accessible to libraries, students, independent scholars, and readers of all ages.

For our initial release we have created seven robust collections to form one the world's most comprehensive catalogs of 18th century works.

Initial Gale ECCO Print Editions collections include:

History and Geography
Rich in titles on English life and social history, this collection spans the world as it was known to eighteenth-century historians and explorers. Titles include a wealth of travel accounts and diaries, histories of nations from throughout the world, and maps and charts of a world that was still being discovered. Students of the War of American Independence will find fascinating accounts from the British side of conflict.

Social Science

Delve into what it was like to live during the eighteenth century by reading the first-hand accounts of everyday people, including city dwellers and farmers, businessmen and bankers, artisans and merchants, artists and their patrons, politicians and their constituents. Original texts make the American, French, and Industrial revolutions vividly contemporary.

Medicine, Science and Technology

Medical theory and practice of the 1700s developed rapidly, as is evidenced by the extensive collection, which includes descriptions of diseases, their conditions, and treatments. Books on science and technology, agriculture, military technology, natural philosophy, even cookbooks, are all contained here.

Literature and Language

Western literary study flows out of eighteenth-century works by Alexander Pope, Daniel Defoe, Henry Fielding, Frances Burney, Denis Diderot, Johann Gottfried Herder, Johann Wolfgang von Goethe, and others. Experience the birth of the modern novel, or compare the development of language using dictionaries and grammar discourses.

Religion and Philosophy

The Age of Enlightenment profoundly enriched religious and philosophical understanding and continues to influence present-day thinking. Works collected here include masterpieces by David Hume, Immanuel Kant, and Jean-Jacques Rousseau, as well as religious sermons and moral debates on the issues of the day, such as the slave trade. The Age of Reason saw conflict between Protestantism and Catholicism transformed into one between faith and logic -- a debate that continues in the twenty-first century.

Law and Reference

This collection reveals the history of English common law and Empire law in a vastly changing world of British expansion. Dominating the legal field is the *Commentaries of the Law of England* by Sir William Blackstone, which first appeared in 1765. Reference works such as almanacs and catalogues continue to educate us by revealing the day-to-day workings of society.

Fine Arts

The eighteenth-century fascination with Greek and Roman antiquity followed the systematic excavation of the ruins at Pompeii and Herculaneum in southern Italy; and after 1750 a neoclassical style dominated all artistic fields. The titles here trace developments in mostly English-language works on painting, sculpture, architecture, music, theater, and other disciplines. Instructional works on musical instruments, catalogs of art objects, comic operas, and more are also included.

The BiblioLife Network

This project was made possible in part by the BiblioLife Network (BLN), a project aimed at addressing some of the huge challenges facing book preservationists around the world. The BLN includes libraries, library networks, archives, subject matter experts, online communities and library service providers. We believe every book ever published should be available as a high-quality print reproduction; printed on-demand anywhere in the world. This insures the ongoing accessibility of the content and helps generate sustainable revenue for the libraries and organizations that work to preserve these important materials.

The following book is in the "public domain" and represents an authentic reproduction of the text as printed by the original publisher. While we have attempted to accurately maintain the integrity of the original work, there are sometimes problems with the original work or the micro-film from which the books were digitized. This can result in minor errors in reproduction. Possible imperfections include missing and blurred pages, poor pictures, markings and other reproduction issues beyond our control. Because this work is culturally important, we have made it available as part of our commitment to protecting, preserving, and promoting the world's literature.

GUIDE TO FOLD-OUTS MAPS and OVERSIZED IMAGES

The book you are reading was digitized from microfilm captured over the past thirty to forty years. Years after the creation of the original microfilm, the book was converted to digital files and made available in an online database.

In an online database, page images do not need to conform to the size restrictions found in a printed book. When converting these images back into a printed bound book, the page sizes are standardized in ways that maintain the detail of the original. For large images, such as fold-out maps, the original page image is split into two or more pages

Guidelines used to determine how to split the page image follows:

• Some images are split vertically; large images require vertical and horizontal splits.
• For horizontal splits, the content is split left to right.
• For vertical splits, the content is split from top to bottom.
• For both vertical and horizontal splits, the image is processed from top left to bottom right.

Albion's GLORY:

A Pindarique

ODE

ON THE

Royal Train

That Attended the Happy

CORONATION

OF

Her moſt Sacred MAJESTY

QUEEN ANN.

Written by the Authors of *Britannia's* Loſs.

LONDON:

Printed and Sold by *John Nutt* near *Stationers-Hall.* 1702.

Albion's GLORY:

A Pindarique

O D E

ON THE

Royal Train

That Attended the Happy

CORONATION, &c.

I.

A Rife my Mufe, thy Sable Weeds throw by;
    And Deck thy felf all Flourifhing and Gay,
    Like fome fair Bride upon her Marriage-Day;
And time thy Lyre to fon'rous Notes of Joy;
Let ev'ry Fibre feel the Influence,
And Blifs dilated Ravifh ev'ry Senfe,
    Let Pleafure trill thro' ev'ry Vein,
    And mighty Tranfports make their way
    Thro' Deluges of Mortal Pain,
    And Taft of Heav'n without Delay ;
See all the little Gaudy Cherubes fly
And draw the Azure Curtains of the Sky;

A

And

And clap their Wings to view the Triumphs of this Glorious
    The Seraphs too in Crouds appear,   (Day:
  And with their Brightnefs Gild our Hemifphere ;
  See, See how they Difplay their Beams around,
  And all the *Angels* ftand prepar'd to found.

II.

Behold the mighty She on whom thefe Gloiies wait,
  The Queen appears in all her Pomp and State,
  At whofe approach the Warlike Mufick Sounds,
  At whofe approach each Heart leaps up with Joy,
  The Banners wave, the Flags and Streamers play,
  Heaven takes the Echo and again Rebounds,
  To Solemnize this Great and Happy Day ;
    And now the foft Flutes in Confort joyn,
  And bands of hovering *Cupids* ftreight repair,
And with their Wings they divide the yielding *Air*,
   To *Bask* and *Revel* here in Rays Divine,
    That Dart from Eyes of *Britifh* Dames,
    And ev'ry wondering Youth Inflames,
    And he who only came to Gaze,
   Is caught in *Beauties* brighteft Maze
     And back returns in Chains ;
In vain he ftrives to taft his wonted Reft,
Nor can with all his force Diflodge th' Imperious Queft.

III.

Be Bold, my Mufe, mount to thofe Realms of Light,
  Take, here and there, a Scetch of Natures Pride,
   But no where fix thy dazled Sight,
   Too weak thy Senfe, their Beams too bright ;
Let Ravifh'd Fancy lead thee on, without the Learned's Guide,
    Strive not to Imitate
   The *Heralds* Rules, or Rules of State,
   But think what *Beauty* ftruck thy Eye,
   Or dwelt upon thy Memory,
   And what thy Soul elated moft
   There lay out all thy Pains and Coft ;

For who can Travel thro' the Region of the Sky,
　And not be Dazled with a flight so high;
Who can diftinctly paint the Starry Galaxy !
　On then, my Mufe, why doft thou fear,
They're fure like *Angels* good, who are like *Angels* fair.

IV.

SOMERSET Fam'd, the Good and Virtuous too,
　　The Train Supports,
How is fhe pleas'd the little Nymphs to view,
　That help the Royal Robe to bear,
　　To fee her Darlings there,
Which will with them become the Pride of Courts,
Chaft as the Buds of Rofes, e're the Air
　Has touch'd their Sweets or wanton'd there,
Does this great Lady and thefe Nymphs appear;
Great ORMOND's Dutchefs, Queen of Beauty, moves,
A Thoufand little *Cupids* watching nigh,
That Shoot their Pointed Arrows from her Eye,
　And each Spectator owns he Loves:
But ah fond Youths, fupprefs your Amourous Flame,
For fhe is one of Chaft *Diana's* Train:
Then Graceful BURLINGTON with ev'ry Virtue Shines,
　A Happy Mother and a Faithful Wife;
　　Here Love with Loyalty Combines,
The two Choice Bleffings of a Married Life;
Alike they both our Love and wonder raife,
Alike they Merit our Eternal Praife.

V.

GRAFTON in Hereditary Honours dreft
　Maintains the undifputed Prize,
　And Darts frefh Glories from her Eyes,
That fills with Killing Pleafures ev'ry Breath,
　Heav'ns bare Idea, Tranfports give,
But none the *Brightnefs* can behold and live:
　Next fair SAINT ALBONS ftrikes the fight
　　With Wonder and Delight,

She

She Treads with such Majeſtick Grace
As Suits her Place,
And well Maintains the Honours of her Antient Race:

VI.

See BOULTON's Dutcheſs moves in State,
Her Charms ſtrike ſure as Fate,
They ſuch reſiſtleſs Flames Diſpence,
Such Univerſal Influence,
Againſt their Pointed Rays there's no Defence:
Now lovely HIDE Appears,
Angelick Brightneſs in her form ſhe wears,
Paradice, none can Copy as they ought,
That, and you are above the Poets Thought;
Well may we doubt where to begin,
Whether with Face, or Shape, or Mein,
Each part deſerves our Praiſes moſt,
We're in a Maze of Beauty loſt,
Oh ! In what Words ſhall I diſcloſe
This Blooming Roſe,
Fair FERRAS whom the Graces all Adorn,
Gay as the Spring, Bright as the Bluſhing Morn,
Had *Paris* whom the Gods Eſteem'd ſo wiſe,
To make him Judge between the Deities,
If theſe three Charmers he had view'd,
The Prize had undecided been,
For each his Judgment had ſubdu'd,
And each the Raviſh'd Youth acknowledg'd Beauties Queen.

VII.

MARLBOROUGH and her lovely Race
The Triumphs Grace,
Wou'd Nature freſh Supplies of *Beauties* make,
From them ſhe muſt the Model take,
Such were the Nymphs when Angels deign'd

To

To mix with Mortals here below,
Such the Seraphick Sons Inflam'd,
But no such Guilt their Souls have Stain'd,
Their Fame's as White as Flakes of falling Snow.
   Here Rank Great FRETSWELL, Chaft and Good,
The Noble Huntrefs of each Field and Wood,
When with Great ANNA fhe purfues the Courfe,
How well fhe Guides, with Dext'rous Arm, the Swift Un-
Lov'd by her Miftrifs, by the People Prais'd, (ruly *Horfe*;
To Greater Dignities may fhe be Rais'd,
High as her utmoft Wifhes can Afcend,
     For fhe'l Difpence
     The Influence,
Oh ! May fhe higher Rife, but ne're from what fhe is, Defcend;
For none's more Worthy to be made a Friend.

VIII.

Behold Bright RUTLAND's Charming Mein and Grace,
   Where e're fhe Walks, Adorns the Place,
   With more than *Britifh* Honours Crown'd,
In her there's *Roman* Grandeur found ;
Within a Caftle Large and Great,
     Fit for her State,
   She like a Queen does live ;
And as the Sun his Beams beftow,
Her Goodnefs Shines on all below,
So High her Station's fix'd by Fate,
No Glories could Addition make,
Heaven Lufture lends to all beneath, but none can take:
   Then Crew behold, the Beautious, Fair,
   And Good, as Guardian Angels are ;
Her Lord with double Honours Shines,
   The Temporal Rank, and Rank Divine,
Here Piety with Mortal Glories joyn ;
   Long may they live, and love,
   May they on Earth no Sorrows know,
   But as in Union here below,
     So may they Reign above.

IX.

IX.

And now the Charming Brides appear
 Beautious, young and Gay,
Like the aproaching Month of *May* ;
See WARRINGTON and PAWLET there,
Each does fair *Flora* Reprefent,
If we at Natures Art may guefs,
 'Tis certain She defign'd no lefs,
When to our World the Charming Nymphs fhe fent :
Mark how the Bridegrooms Eyes their Steps purfue,
 And fain would keep 'em ftill in view,
 To Gaze upon their World of Charms;
And think the Prize is Deftin'd for their Arms :
ASHBENHAM's Princely Dowry was by Fate beftow'd
 To be imenfly Good,
 The Rural Swains around her Crowd,
Her Favours Taft, and Sing her Praife aloud ;
True Generofity in Noble Pomp fhe bears,
 And well deferves the Honours which fhe wears.

X.

WHARTON the Airy, Brisk, and Gay,
A Thoufand Graces round her Play,
For her each Swain Admiring dies,
And falls a willing Sacrifice,
While with Bewitching Art,
Her Beauty Wounds the Eye, her Air and Wit, the Heart :
 Next her Friend
 The Rites Attend,
The Charming CROMWELL Claims a Part,
Whole *Hecatombs* fhe leads in Chains,
Unconquer'd yet the Beautious Maid remains:
 CARTWRIGHT makes the Triumverate,
To none Inferior or in *Birth* or *Fate* ;
 She's Fruitful as the fpreading Vine,
 Her Off-Spring like the Stars do fhine,
Which when fhe fees, a pleafing Joy her Cheeks or'e fpread,
To them fhe gives her Love, and knows no fecond Bed.

XI.

Now, my Muse, prepare
To Sing of an unequal'd Fair,
Prepare to Celebrate her Wit,
    Yet, Oh ! Be ware,
For she's a Judge of it ;
'Tis there that Genius doth Survive,
That in her Father kept the World Alive ;
    On him did ev'ry Muse attend,
Now ev'ry Muse to SANDWICH is a Friend,
    On her the Graces smile,
And SANDWICH they Proclaim the Sapho of our Isle :
    See PEMBROOK's Countess, Juno-like, she moves
        With ev'ry Vertue fraught,
    Oh Guard her all ye Chaster Loves,
By her let ev'ry *British* Wife be Taught,
Her Pious Life by all the World Ador'd,
Only belov'd, and loving of her Lord.

XII.

On the Royal Charge does SCARBOROUGH wait,
SCARBOROUGH the Illustrious and the Great,
    First bright MARIA's Court she Grac'd,
    Again she's in the Circle Plac'd,
    Her Godlike Mistriss knows to Chuse,
Nor wou'd she such a faithful Servant lose :
CRAVEN and CORNWALLIS, new Raptures bring,
Oh my Charm'd Muse, when wilt thou end thy Song ?
    Thou art bewilder'd in the Beautious Throng,
Yet, these two lovely Dames, who can forbear to Sing,
        Who can forbear to raise
        Eternal Altars to their Praise ?
Behold their lovely Mein, their Charming Grace,
        Each has an Angels Face,
    Their Tracts of Light Gilds all the Place.

XIII.

Here ſtop, my Muſe, the Gallant ORMOND view,
   See how he moves with awful Grace,
   Clad in the *Honours* of his Race;
He both Inherits and Deſerves 'em too;
   In Action, like the God of War,
   In Peace, he's Calm and Smooth,
   Such Sweetneſs in his Looks appear,
   Juſt ſuch a Mein and ſuch an Air
     As ſuits the *God* of *Love*;
Thy Royal Miſtriſs ſees thy Worth, and knows
Princes ſuch Noble Actions ſhou'd Reward,
By what ſhe'as given, ſhe already ſhows
True Valour ſhall not paſs without Regard;
Yet may ſhe raiſe thee to a Nobler height,
For none more Worthy on her Favours wait;
And here three *Graceful Royal* Figures ſtand,
St. ALBANS, RICHMOND, and NORTHUMBERLAND,
Their Father's Image in each Face appears,
   And each his Port Majeſtick wears;
   The People gaze with new delight,
And think their once Lov'd Monarch is again in ſight.

VII.

Illuſtrious BEDFORD, *High* and *Great*,
 Does on his Royal Sovereign wait,
Englands High Conſtable for this bleſt Day,
Too large a Power to bear a longer Date,
   The Poſt by him ſo Nobly Grac'd,
   All wiſh the Place might lag,
   To whoſe Dread Sway
The whole admiring World would willing *Homage* pay;
   A *Prince* with thouſand Vertues ſtor'd,
Juſt to his Honour, Sacred is his Word,
Mæcena of my Muſe, my Patron Lord.
Advance, my Muſe, aſpiring Pen advance,
Let glorious DEVONSHIRE *Adorn* thy Song,
   To Sing his *Fame* will thine enhance.

The *Admir'd Hero* of the shining Throng,
A Grace to Courts, of ev'ry Nymph the Pride,
   To please our Eyes and wound our Hearts ;
How oft is *Cupid's* Bow drawn on his side ?
How oft he strikes with Thousand, Thousand Darts,
Like Kings he looks, yet soft as smiling loves,
His Words as smooth as Downe of Feather'd Doves ;
   Oh ! how shall I this Subject quit,
   When I reflect upon his Wit,
   Upon his Charms and ev'ry Grace
    That wantons in his Face ;
The Task's too great, in vain IV'e strung my Lyre,
So what I can't describe, must silently Admire.
Great NORMANBY, and DORSET, each *Appolo's* Darling Son,
  VVhose Names to after Ages will endure,
  From Envious Criticks, and their Rage secure,
  Their Stren'ous Muse is equall'd yet by none,
  For Policy and Judgment both Renown'd,
  And ever Loyal to their Country found,
  May all their VVishes in this Reign be Crown'd.

       XV.

  Next PETERBOROUGH's Sense,
Judicious Wit, and Eloquence,
   Our Senate have allow'd
To be the most Polite and Fine,
That e're in Mortal Man did shine,
   Or Heaven yet bestow'd ;
   Had he been born
When *Roman* Heroes did the World Adorn,
He had undisputed Consular Honours worn.
  HALIFAX the *Mœcenus* of our Time,
   Which way shall I describe
The Poet's Patron, and the Muses Pride,
Oh ! how shall I his Gallant worth define ?
With Learn'd Expressions I'm too weakly Fraught,
We should have *Virgil's* Pen, to Paint thee as we ought ;
   Thy Virtue still, like some great Star
   That spight of darkning Clouds appear,
    In Heaven fixt
  Nor can with base Allay be mixt,   (more Clear.
But throws the thick wrought Curtain off, and shines again

XVI.

Now, now, my Muse, the Gen'rous SCARSDALE Paint,
    Draw him Great, Good, and Juft,
      His Life no Treafonous Crimes can Taint,
There's none can fay he e're betray'd his Truft;
No Man's by him Defrauded of his Due,
    No Trader Broke, or forc'd to Fly,
    No Bills unpaid, neglected lie;
Mean Acts like thefe, can ne're his Soul fubdue,
    He's Courteous, Affable and Free,
      As one fo Great can be,
And to his Word and Honour ever True.
PEMBROOK, thy Miftrifs's Guardian Shield,
VVhofe Right it is the Sword to bear,
That knows fo well to manage it in War;
In Councils VVife, Bold and Couragious in the Field;
    Great Neptune and the Sea *Gods* all Rejoyce,
    Curle their blue Locks, and on the Billows Ride,
    Longing to fee their VVatry Oceans Pride,
To Crown him Victor with a general Voice.
    Affift *Appolo*, and ye Mufes Nine,
Like to my Subject, let my Verfes Shine,
Home ev'ry God inftruct my feeble Pen,
Cow to defcribe the very Beft of Men,
A Man whofe Afpect might the Chafteft move,
And make her foft and plyable to Love;
A Man whofe grateful Nature, and whofe Wit
    Admiration does beget;
From Noble blood the *Hero* fprings,
Has all the Worth that Poets fain in Kings,
His God-like Acts are Echo'd round by Fame,
By thefe faint hints, the World will guefs his Name.

XVII.

BURLINGTON adds Lufture to the Noble Train,
    His Looks have fuch Majeftick Grace,
    Yet foft as an *Arcadian* Swain,
Eternal Sweetnefs Revels in his Face,
He's Brave and Gen'rous to the laft Degree,

And a true Pattern of Nobility.

The Favo'rite of our late lov'd Monarch, fee
Great ALBERMARLE, that lovely Youth,
Fam'd for his Loyalty and Truth,
The wond'rous Pattern of Fidelity.
WINCHELCY, well became the Honours of the Day,
Fresh Glories still, may ANNA give,
Each Muse for thee shall Tune her lay,
And to Posterity thy Name shall live ;
You search their Sacred Stors and learnings World Survey,
To you they must their Grateful Tribute pay.
ANGLESEY the Young, the Gay, the Brave,
A Noble Youth from Headlong Passion free,
And to no Vice a Slave;
Lord of himself, at perfect Liberty ;
Thy Vertues still shall rise and live, v
For in no Soil can Glory better thrive ;
On then, in Honours Race,
Till Laurel Wreaths thy sprightly *Temples Grace*,
Till the loud *Trump* of *Fame*
Shall to Posterity transmit thy Name.
CHOLMUNDEY, next, of Noble Worth,
And RADNOR too,
Both set the Triumphs forth,
And make compleat the glorious VIEW;
For ever may they Shine in State,
Whilst Abler Pens than mine, their Noble Lives Relate:
And now the Glorious Prince behold,
Majestick are his Eyes,
How oft he turns them back upon the lovely *Prize*,
On her who wears the Sacred Gold,
With Husband's Kindness and the Lover's Care,
He watches the Illustrious Fair,
Guard 'em ye *Powers*, from all Malignant Stars,
And Crown with Conquest all their VVars ;
Numerous Beauties yet remain in Store,   (more.
But having Nam'd the Royal Pair, my Muse will Sing no

F I N I S.

CPSIA information can be obtained
at www.ICGtesting.com
Printed in the USA
BVHW011236280819
556948BV00029B/94/P